Father Kissmass and Mother Claws

17137.

£5-
ged

FATHER KISSMASS AND MOTHER CLAWS

BEL MOONEY
GERALD SCARFE

HAMISH HAMILTON · LONDON

Father Kissmass and Mother Claws lived in a big, grand House in the far and frozen north of the world. They had no children, but lived with their trusty herd of pet tamedeer (the old breed, *Empi Torioses*), who waited patiently in their stalls for their day of freedom, whilst Mother Claws's favourite guard dogs, Tebbie and Hestle, snapped and snarled outside.

Mother Claws was a stern mistress. She ruled her House, the tamedeer, her dogs, and above all she ruled Father Kissmass, with an iron rod. The only things she could not rule were the dreams which haunted her nights – dreams of sinking ships, of rending earthquakes; dreams peopled with nameless howling shadows coming closer and closer . . .

She would wake in a fury. "I'll hammer them small, I'll grind them to pieces, I'll trim their edges for them," she hissed, grasping at the empty air. But she quickly forgot those dreams. She put on her best blue fur, picked up her handbag, and strode off to Market. There she terrified the foreign traders by clawing back everything she paid them, and by scratching out the items on other people's shopping lists, with a wild cackle of "Out! Out!" And that was how she got her name.

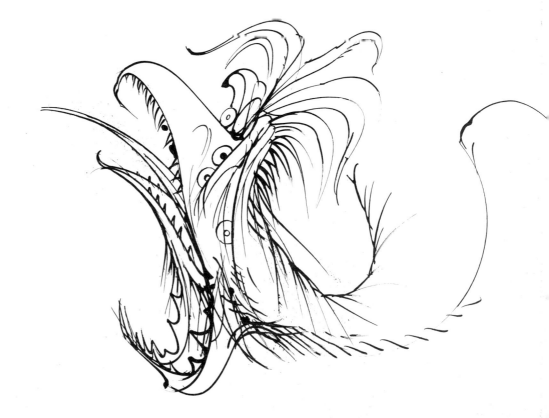

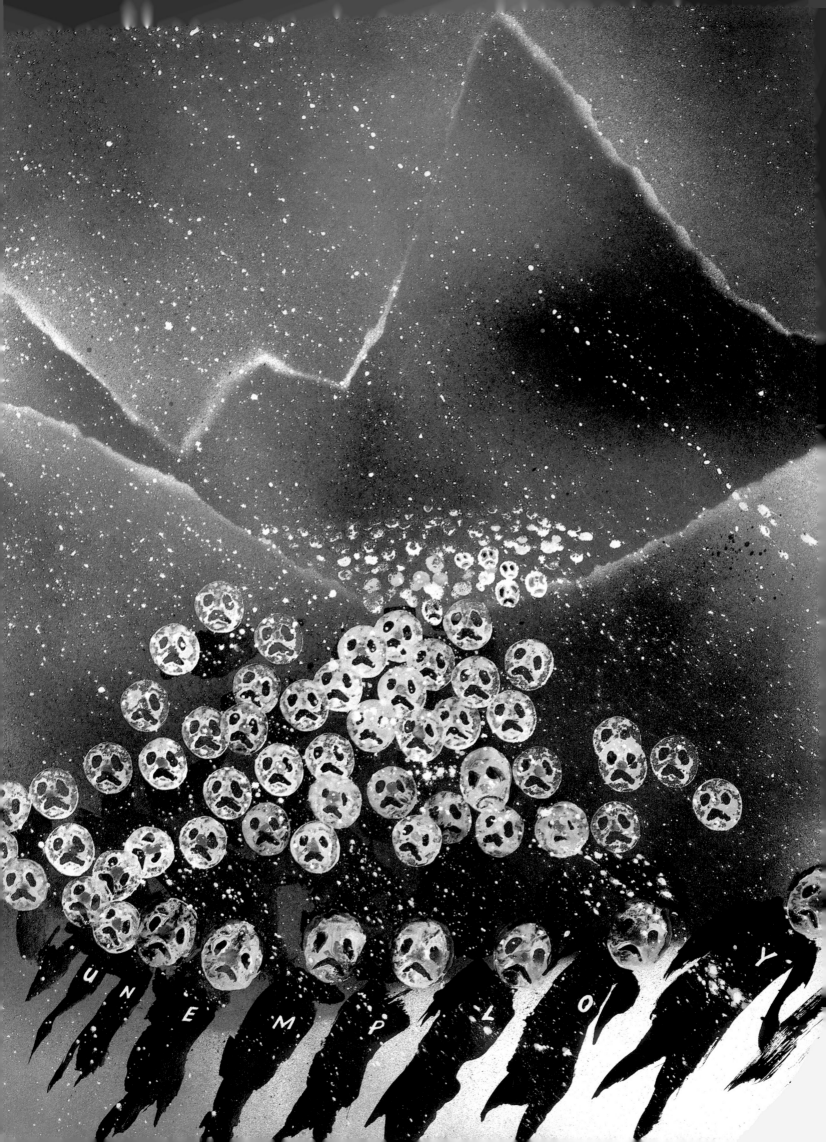

Mother Claws firmly believed that everything she believed was firm, and that she was destined to be the mother of a great nation. But her nation often made her sad, and then tears of disappointment would well in her blue eyes. The tamedeer would cry too. "Mummy's *triste*!" they would howl in franglais, "Mummy *triiiiiste*." Their tears formed a large pool which froze in the chill blast of Mother Claws's sighs, and she pointed at it, saying it was impossible to do any turns there without falling over. So it was that her grief began a whole philosophy that the tamedeer called mummytrism.

There was one secret ambition Mother Claws had which only Father Kissmass knew. She yearned for the day when she could swap the old red sleigh, with its silly jingling bells, for a queenly coach. She imagined a time when her tamedeer would pull her through the streets, and she would wave on this side and on that, to her cheering, devoted people. But Father Kissmass reminded her that she often told others not to set their sights too high, not to want what could not possibly be theirs. Those words made Mummy *trister* than ever, and she warned him savagely that he must tighten his own belt a few more notches, before the spring.

Now that was something old Father Kissmass found very hard to do, for he was very fat and rather greedy. He also had some rather strange habits. For instance, when people wrote him little letters asking for the things they most needed, he would chortle, "Ho, ho, ho – it's kissmass time again!", and turn his back on them. Which is how he got his name.

When the children and their parents got no response, they wrote to the tamedeer instead, and one by one the poor dumb beasts filed in to see him, holding the notes in their hooves and hinting that perhaps he might take notice . . .? Then Father Kissmass would part his full red lips, and dribble with excitement as he lashed them hard, yelling, "Take vat! And vat! And vat!" Gradually the tamedeer learned to love the whips, and the forgotten letters piled up in their stalls until the cruel winter wind blew them across the land, like snow.

One year Father Kissmass and Mother Claws were preparing themselves for their annual task of putting something in the stockings of the nation. They did not like it at all. In fact it made them most bad-tempered. Father Kissmass peered dubiously into the family purse, whilst Mother Claws opened her kitchen cabinet. "Not much there," she screeched, "this cabinet's even emptier than usual. We'll have to cut back this year."

Father Kissmass hopped from one stout leg to the other. "Oh goody," he squeaked with glee. "I'll go and get the scissors. Can I make the first cut, Mother?"

"No!" said Mother Claws, as she always did.

"Oh, please, please!" he begged. "I'll make it just where you say."

"Well, there's no alternative, is there?" she replied coldly, slamming the cupboard door.

They unrolled a map of the country on the kitchen table, and studied it with care. Mother Claws smiled grimly. "Yorkshire's definitely out," she said.

"Yorkshire gone!" trilled Father Kissmass as he went snip, snip.

"And Wales," she said.

"Wales gone – snip, snip!" he echoed.

"And Kent," she said.

"Kent gone – snip, snip!" he echoed.

"Scotland too, of course," she added.

"Och aye!" he grinned.

So they went on, until the map was a pattern of gaping holes, especially at the top. Mother Claws narrowed her eyes. "You could cut out a few stockings in Whitehall, and in Cheltenham," she hissed.

"None for the uncivil servants!" shrieked Father K. "And none for Oxford, either, Mother!"

"We won't go to Liverpool," breathed Mother Claws, closing her eyes for a second with deep and painful emotion.

"Yes, Liverpool, cut, cut!" Father Kissmass sang out as the scissors did their work.

"No stockings for Ireland, of course," she added, "unless we fill them full of potatoes!" At that Father Kissmass could barely cut for laughing.

At last the map looked a very sorry sight, the country in rags and tatters – but Mother Claws was pleased. "That's what we call good housekeeping," she said.

"We?" he asked, turning his round, foolish face to her.

"Idiot! Don't you know that *We* means Me! ME! ME!" she screamed, driving him from the room.

Because they were late in getting the tamedeer ready, carelessly they let out the first ones who trotted forward, leaving the rest to wait their turn next year. But, as they were hitching them to the sleigh, they heard a low murmuring from the back. And to their astonishment the red-nosed tamedeer, who used to lead the herd, spoke up. He said that some of the beasts did not like to think of so many empty stockings in the land. "You won't go down in history – you're finished!" jeered Mother Claws, turning her back to climb into the almost-empty sleigh. Then Father Kissmass yelled, "Silence!", and cut across their backs with his whip as they galloped up and over the snow.

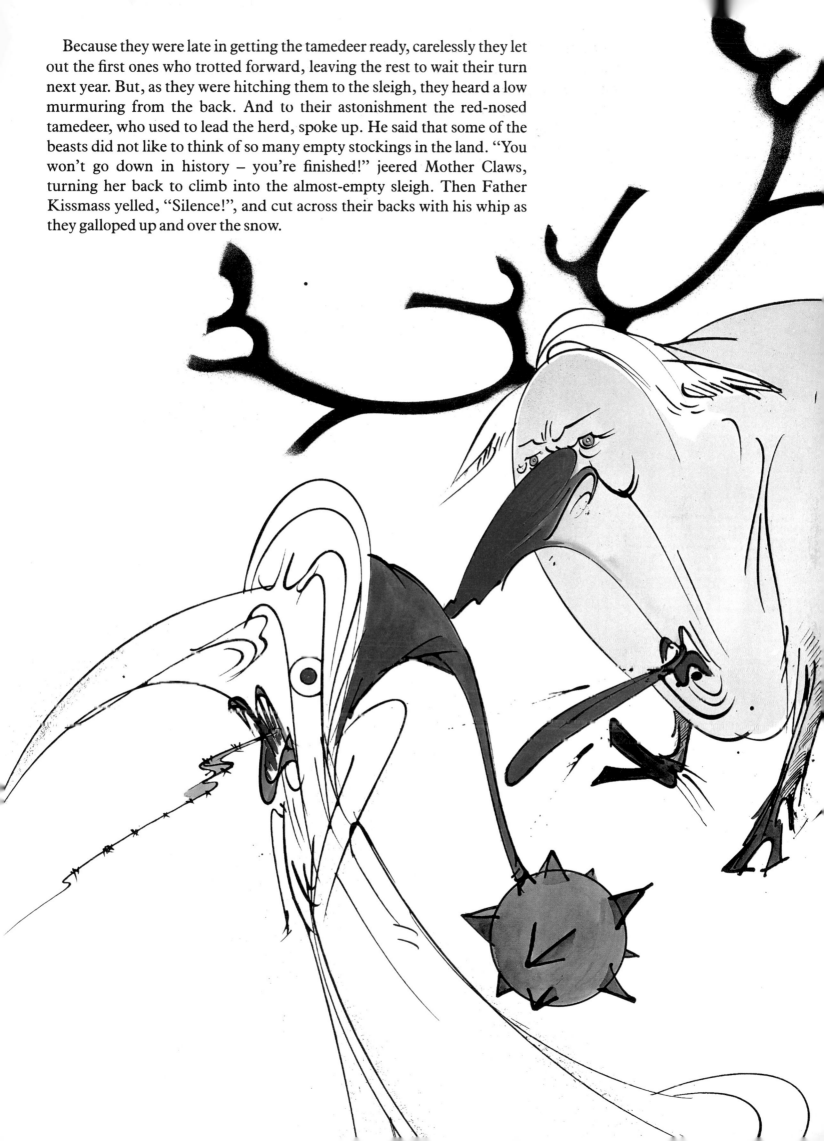

It did not take long to fill the few stockings in the pleasant places they had left on their map. Largely, finely woven ones of silk and cashmere hung beside wide fireplaces of elegant stone or marble, which could accommodate even a girth as wide as Father K's. And there were cut-glass nips of brandy left for the portly visitor, who vowed to Mother Claws that he would give them more than a million presents next year, in gratitude. "Yes, dear, these are *our* people," smiled Mother Claws, weaving tinsel in her hair for joy.

It was when Father K and Mother C thought their job was over for another year, that the astonishing thing happened. The tamedeer rebelled. Instead of obeying the order to head for home, they turned sharp left, and no amount of whip-cracking would stop them. Over distant lands and seas of imagination they flew, losing track of time, until at last the sleigh landed on a low, shabby flat roof.

"Where are we?" whispered Mother Claws.

"Look – there's a star up there I don't recognise," mused Father Kissmass.

"Then it must be an awards ceremony," hissed Mother Claws, patting her hair into place.

The red-nosed tamedeer led them all down some steps and into the mean building, past strange animals dozing in the dirt who made queer grunting sounds as they slept. Huddled together at the back of the stable a young man and woman gazed at the visitors with sad and gentle eyes, and gestured mutely towards the baby, lying in the straw at their feet.

"Who are they?" mumbled Father Kissmass, sweating under his fur hood and false beard, for he was not used to warmth.

"They have no home," said the first tamedeer.

"The baby needs special treatment but the hospital lacks equipment and, besides, the list is long," said the second tamedeer.

"The father has bicycled all over the countryside looking for work, but no one wants a jobbing carpenter," said the third tamedeer.

"They have no money for food," said the fourth tamedeer.

"Nor clothes, nor presents," said the fifth.

"They are close to despair," said the red-nosed tamedeer, "so are there no tidings of comfort you can bring to them in this season of goodwill, Father Kissmass and Mother Claws?"

At that moment a crowd of women, all dressed in white, appeared around the family, holding up candles which filled the stable with golden light as they sang, "Peace on earth, goodwill to all people. Peace on earth, peace. . . ."

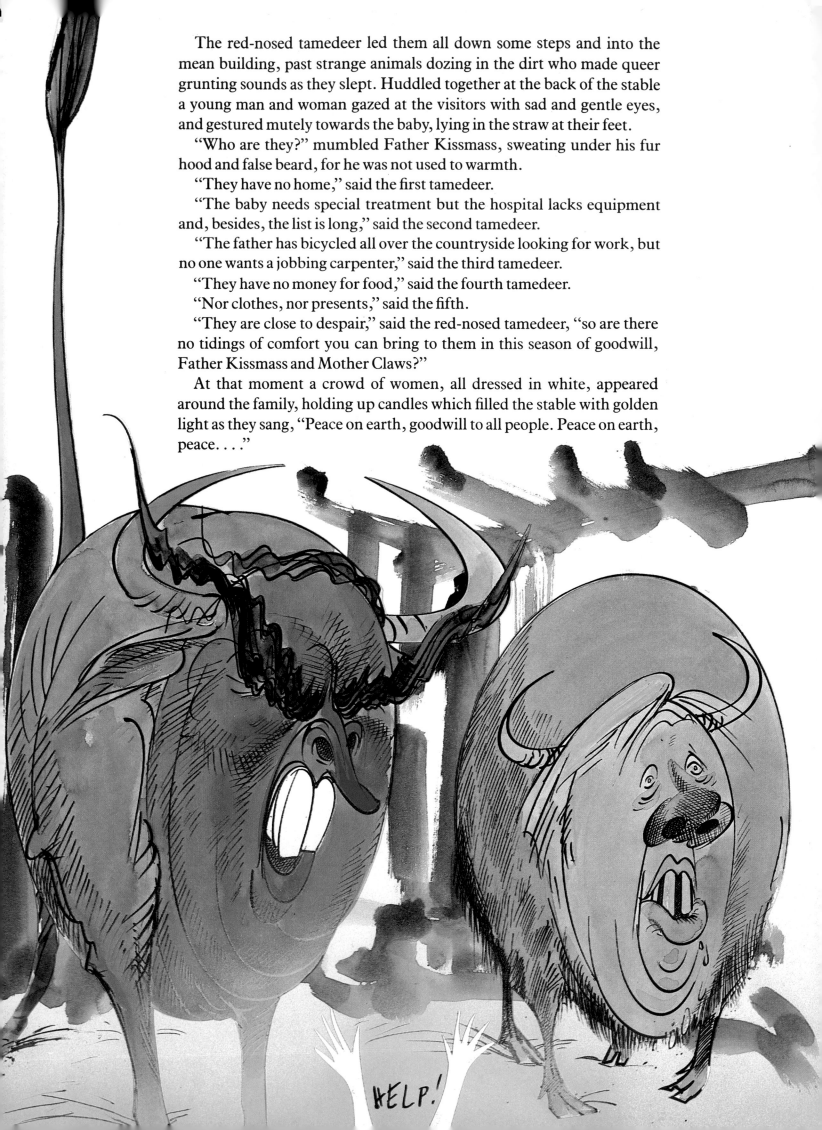

HELP!

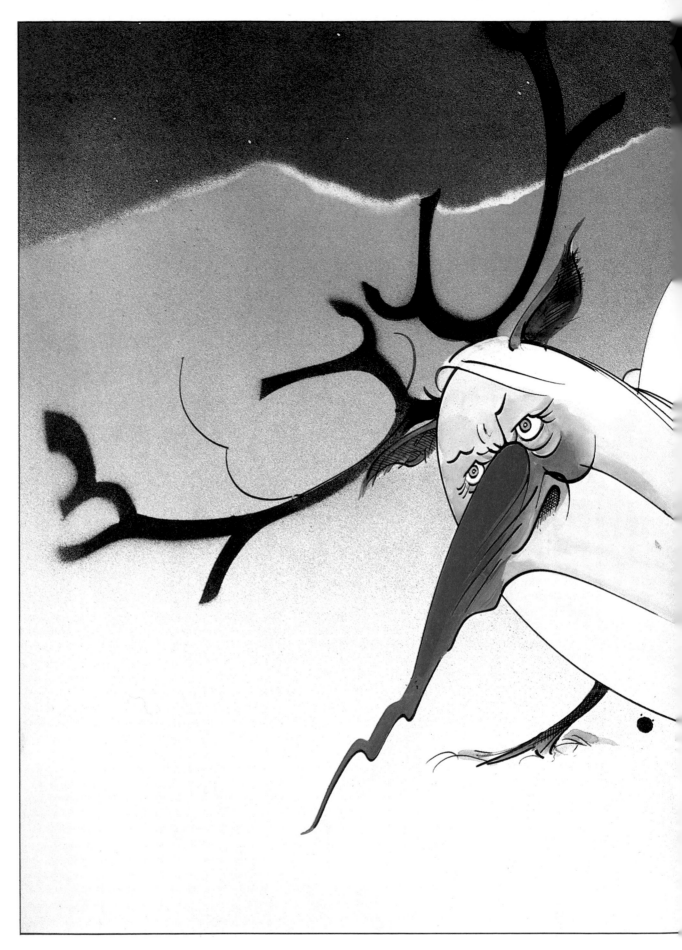

Then Mother Claws turned pale. "Just as I thought! It's the enemy within. Troublemakers! Dupes!" she snarled, and whirled on the red-nosed tamedeer in her fury. "You! I can tell it by the colour of your nose! And your little wet eyes! Call yourself an *Empus Toriosis*? You can stay with these common farm animals. You're not coming back with ME!"

And she would not listen to the pleading of the mother as she held up

her child, nor would she see the loving expression in that child's eye.
Instead, she kicked red-nose out of the way, drove the other tamedeer
back to the sleigh, and hauled Father Kissmass after her. Not trusting
anyone now, she took the reins herself to drive home through the
dangerous, starry wastes. Left behind in the stable, the lowly creatures
mooed reproach at the abandoned tamedeer, who drooped his head in
shame. "I tried" was all he could say.

When the jingling sleigh reached the House once more, the tamedeer were quivering with fear in their harnesses. Tebbie and Hestle sensed it, and dripped rabid saliva as they changed their welcoming yelps to low snarls of warning. Inside the stable block the rest of the herd whimpered softly, scenting terror in the air.

Then one rebel tamedeer moved up and apologised to Mother Claws for the mistaken revolt. As for the rest, they stared at the frozen wastes to which she pointed, glanced toward the stalls they knew to be warm and safe, each with its bucket of steaming mash . . . and they sank to their knees. "Yes, I will forgive you – just this once," crooned Mother Claws, as she counted them into the stables. "But you must always remember that Mother knows best."

"Ho, ho, ho!" laughed Father Kissmass as he closed the kitchen door behind them, and poured himself a large glass of port. "They'll learn, Mother . . . They'll cut their cloth according to their vote."

"Mmmm, cut . . . cut . . ." Mother Claws had picked up the scissors, and was sharpening them thoughtfully, a manic gleam in her eye. "I could dock some tails, and thin some antlers," she whispered. Glancing coldly at the brimming glass of port she added, "And *you*, Father K, you're much too fat, you could do with a trim . . ."

So the tamedeer's rebellion ended there, that Christmas. And the land was still in the grip of the harshest, most unrelenting winter for years and years.

First published in Great Britain 1985
by Hamish Hamilton Ltd
Garden House 57-59 Long Acre London WC2E 9JZ

British Library Cataloguing in Publication Data

Mooney, Bel
   Father Kissmass and Mother Claws.
   I. Title   II. Scarfe, Gerald
   823′.914[F]   PR6063.058/

   ISBN 0-241-11695-3
   ISBN 0-241-11700-3 Pbk

Typeset by Rowland Phototypesetting (London) Ltd
Printed in Great Britain by
Redwood Burn Ltd, Trowbridge, Wiltshire